COSMIC HEARTS

Poetry from the Soul

ARABELLA CROOKESHAW

Arabella Crookeshaw Publishing

Contents

PART TWO: UNQUESTIONED ANSWERS

PART THREE: THE ENDING THAT CAME

PART FOUR: THE BEGINNING TO COME

EPILOGUE

COSMIC HEARTS

To the man who broke my heart, and inspired me deeply.

Part One: Unanswered Questions

A STORY OF LOSS

infinite worlds

In a world of possibilities,
With infinite parallel dimensions,
And the simultaneous occurrence of everything and every reality,

With infinite realms in which we made it,
in which I woke up next to you this morning,
in which you would answer if I called,
in which you couldn't live without me.

Infinite worlds where we are together.
Why then, did we have to pick this one?

forbidden

How could a love like ours be forbidden?
Are you afraid of the way we shake the mountaintops,
Of how the crash of my lips reminds you of lightning,
Shocking your soul and leaving you stunned?

Are you afraid of the control I take of you,
When I enter your life like the wind,
And soothe your entire being in a state of temporary bliss,
Of the way I cradle you in my love,
Like a gentle breeze against your skin?

Are you afraid of the glow that surrounds us,
A brightness that rivals the sun,
And warms your cold bones,
And helps you to grow,
As if you were nothing more than a delicate flower?

Are you afraid of the way we change together,
Like seasons moving from hot to cold,
And our emotions from smothering to chilling,
Forever aging within this change,
As we move through each passing day?

Are you afraid of the way the earth quakes when we part,
As if the earth's chest is heaving,
With the agony of such a loss,
Disaster unfolding in my absence?

Are you afraid of the depth of our love,
Deeper and more obscure than the oceans,
Powerful and overwhelming like a hurricane,
And sometimes as still and serene as a pond?

Are you afraid of the way we create life,
A force that is primally human between us,
Forming as carbon just to touch you,
Growing our lives in the soil of our love,
And praying for a fruitful harvest?

How can a love like ours be forbidden?
It's the most natural thing on earth.

again

Again and again,
I will perform this dance with you.
Always taking the same steps,
And the same missteps.

Again and again,
I would bare my heart on my sleeve for you.
Just to have you crumble it in your fist,
And then ask for me to give it again.

Again and again,
I will say that I love you.
Irregardless of the silence that may follow,
Just for a random chance to hear your voice.

Again and again,
I will wait for you to return.
Your love is the sweetest taste that I have ever known,
And every drop is worth my pride.

hurt

You disappeared so suddenly
That the dust did not even settle
From the space you held
A dusty silhouette of the man I loved

So unreachable
That it feels that you were just a daydream
Sometimes a nightmare
But always a paradise

Gaslighting personified
Though it feels like smoke and mirrors
I know that it was real
Only from the pain in my chest

dust

How did I give you so much power over me?
I got so lost in the hazy sweetness that was you
That I don't remember when I dropped my defenses
And now I can't find them
And I need them again.

How could you ask for my heart?
When you had no intentions for it
Just a want for the purpose of obtaining
Just because you could.

How did my walls crumble so completely?
Right before you left me without shelter
Alone in the dust
Before it even had a chance to settle
Falling around me
And leaving me choked.

grey

When I think of you
I think of the color grey
Muted, uninspiring, and cold
Unflavored popcorn
And dust.

Too scared to see the rainbow
Closed away and dark
Never reaching, but never still
Moving in the same full circle
Routine. Sleep. Routine.

You are old while you are young
What does it matter
If your life is just a circle
Routine. Birth. Routine.
Routine. Death. Routine.

I was almost caught in your circle.
Dulled and hazy
In a whirlwind of stillness
My wings almost clipped
And my rainbow extinguished.

But as your cycle renews again
Your monochrome madness
Rejects the rainbow's light
You hide away and face the dark
While my wings are lost in flight.

please (pt 1)

Please give your heart to me.

I am so afraid
That someone else
Will not care for it like I will.

It is so precious
And valuable to me.

What is someone breaks
The one thing that I love the most?

Let me lock your heart away
In my safest keeping
For I can keep it whole
Even better than you can.

my surrender

I fall upon the ground,
and I lay down my arms,
my body, my mind, my soul,
I surrender it all to the void.

To Karma, I give you my pain.
Take it far, take it home, take it to its source.

To Justice, I give you my revenge.
I don't quite care for that any more.

To Wisdom, I give you my confusion.
I do not want to find the meaning of these lessons.

To Chaos, I give you my fears.
I give in to the uncertainty of this world.

To Love, I give you my wounds.
For had I not known beauty, there would be no sense of loss.

To Strength, I give you my insecurities.
For their weight broke my back and did not build my arms.

To Grief, I give you my anger.
I would rather know you as an old friend.

To Bliss, I give you my tears.
They came into the world to fill your absence.

To the Source of all, I lay my ego down and follow your path back
home.

ache

I don't know what to tell my heart anymore
She has heard so many lies
That nothing feels real
The world is impermanent
And promises feel impossible to keep

I want to hold my heart
In ways that you should have
I want to listen to her beat an anguished tone
And emphasize with her anger
Agreeing with her about the predictability of it all

We'll have a glass of red together
Me and my heart
And we'll reminisce about different days
Not better, but a different version of us
When that ache was from abundance

I'll sit here with my heart all night
Holding her and carrying our burdens upon my shoulder
We'll ache all night together
Drunk on heartbreak and romance and wine
My oldest friend

truth

I thought that I knew you
Thought that I had memorized every line on your body
Every note in your laugh
And every dream in your heart

I trusted that you were true
That you were the one that I was meant for
Created to be my companion
Truthful to your core

I needed you to be real
To wear your real heart upon your sleeve
To mean the declarations you made to me
To honor every vow

I wanted your love so badly
To trust that your feelings were real
To know that your tears meant something
Finding meaning in your absence.

missing piece

Two halves of separate puzzles
Broken on their edges and wanting desperately to fit
Each wrong fit taking more
Breaking and warping
Until something different remains

I am everyone's soul mate
But no one truly feels like mine
I'm a skeleton key that works for every door
But will never know where home truly is

I see so much beauty in every soul
But when will someone look at mine
And see the masterpiece that lay beneath
Not an interpretation of what the piece means to them
But true understanding and awe
Of just how it is
Frayed and delicate and glorious

Where is my one, my only
My other half
My missing piece
Perhaps I'm just too whole.

please (pt 2)

Please don't come back to me
Because I don't have the strength to turn you away.

Please hate me in perpetual silence
Because the sound of your voice will be a torture that I cannot bear.

Please stay away and forget my existence
Because maybe your memory will fade too.

Please don't ask for my love again
Because I can't help but to give you every drop of every single thing
I have.

Please start a new life without me
Because I can't start mine while waiting for you to come back.

Please fade away forever from me
Because I can feel your energy even in the smallest increments.

Please never love me again
Because I can't be the one to stop loving you.

miracles

I loved you so much
That my entire earth shook from your lightest touch
That my heart beat in morse code that spelled your name
That angels came down and danced around us
Because we shone a light that rivaled heaven

I loved you so much
That the stardust within us would come alive
And shine twinkles in our eyes
And illuminate our darkness with an ethereal glow
That made the moon jealous and in awe of our intensity

How could I have loved you like that,
And yet, we still ended?

The cosmos will be ever expanding
The earth will always spin
The sun will rise in the east and set in the west
And the universe remains in equilibrium
Because it is built on miracles.

So how does the world keep moving,
When our miracle love stays still?

Part Two:
Unquestioned Answers

A STORY OF REFLECTION

our home among the stars

We exist beyond the ether
in our home among the stars
cuddled closely by the cosmos
deeply intimate but free of physicality
where the laws of our dear Earth do not apply
where religion does not matter and cannot divide
because we know that God moves through us
that the Earth was created
so that we could practice this love
so that we could return to our home among the stars
hand in hand
where fear cannot reach us
and pain has no place
because there, we vibrate with love
and then we choose another life together
another challenge to find you again
another chance to prove our love
not only to the cosmos, but to the Earth too.

muscle memory

I wish I could cry for you
To wash my wounds with salty tears
And flood my system with enough force
To remove your stain entirely

I wish I could scream your name
In agony and as a curse
But the mere whisper of your syllable
Is unutterable in a context that is missing you

I wish I could shed my skin
Because every inch remembers your touch
I wish I could skin my body and start over
But my skin keeps your memory deeply tattooed

I wish I could tell my heart that you never existed
To alter its rhythm so it will stop beating your name
Even if it stopped entirely
But my heart still sings love songs about you

I wish I could hate you with everything in my entire being
But my body is too exhausted to try
I can't erase you from my mind
When my body remembers that you were here

my sunshine

You, my sunshine.
Me, who flew too close to the sun.
Such a fire can burn deeply
When you're only used to the moon
I would gaze upon you until I'm blind
I would let myself fall to cinders
If it meant surrendering
To the warmth of your embrace
You illuminate my every being
Shining a light on my flaws
But also empowering my brilliance
And burning through my soul.

my sweet reflection

To you, my sweet reflection,
You, exactly like me, but in reverse.
You, who sees your own demons in my reflection to you,
who sees the emotions that you avoid in my eyes,
your fears, your insecurities, your mistakes,
the pain in my eyes reflects the pain in yours,
but in reverse.

You, who reflects to me my greatest fears,
my frustrating and anxious attachments,
my endless need to be validated by your reflection,
my painful attempts to see you only within my own reflection,
and inability to see you otherwise,
and in reverse.

Us, who reflect together,
our swollen eyes,
our broken hearts,
our shaky hands,
our desire to crumble and fall apart,
held together, keeping each other solid in our reflections of our-
selves.

I only know you in my own reflection.

breathe

Sometimes I feel that I cannot breathe air
without you in it
As if my body depends on inhaling you
I go into shock without you
Like a fish that wandered out of the ocean
Trapped and dying

And other times I feel like the air feels clearer
without you in it
As if the air is lighter
And without a staleness
A staleness from an old mentality
Stuck in its way and too outdated for this time

This air is different now
Breathable.
As if that fish adapted
And manifested lungs
Evolving without you

marijuana and the
man I love

Marijuana and the man I love,
euphoric feelings, brightened colors,
my chest always feels lighter,
mountaintop sceneries and sandy beaches
never looked better,
I crave you every waking and dreaming moment.

Marijuana and the man I love,
changing my body and my mind,
holding me back from full understanding,
a life built around you is a life that is stuck,
bad habits that I am working to break.

separate

I love the person you are
And despise the person you try to be.

I love the way your laugh bellows
Through a room and through my heart
And despise the way you try to stifle it
Afraid of making noise.

I love the way we act like kids together
Inner children coming out to play
And despise the way that you get so judgmental
When you are perceived by anyone else.

I love the way you make love to me
With your entire heart and soul
And despise the way you treat yourself after
Praying for forgiveness for love.

I love the way we take on the world
Holding hands in infinite cities
And despise the way you stay so far
Separate lives, and a separate man.

her

A lifetime of pain behind your eyes
Reflected like fire in your gaze
Memories of being burned by the world
Moments that sparked the light that you would become
A brilliant fury of passion
My phoenix asleep in embers
Soon to illuminate the sky with her.

My lady divine.
Shaped by the world who tried to smother you
My diamond under the pressure
Growing more beautiful and rare with time
Never cracking from the weight.

You, who exist deeply rooted in the ground
Holding me firmly to the earth with you
Cradled in the love that is her
You have become my home.

I can only exist on this earth with her.
Only here by the grasp in which she holds me
But as my soul drifts toward the clouds
And I look back once more
I realize that it was her
Who always held the earth up.
Never crumbling under its weight.

down the rabbit hole

I'm chasing that high
that weightless nothing
floating through the in between
so far away

take me past the stars
that used to be in my eyes
soaring higher and higher
but never reaching anything
close my eyes to reality
and make me forget

help me fade into nothing
to cease in being
that rabbit hole we fall in
of stars and memories
push me further still
push me to the light

I fall down harder
smoke clears my lungs
reality grips too tight
and I hurt again.

steady hands

In that first moment after spilling wine
When you haven't yet caught your breath
And your thoughts are consumed
By what a mistake you made
By how horrific the stain will be
Dread of the task to come
Anger deflected and bouncing round the room
The feeling that you couldn't possibly handle
Any more spilled glasses of wine

But steady hands craft steady futures
Anxious hands craft anxious futures
Frustrated hands craft frustrating futures

Just pick up the shards of glass.
And clean the stain best you can.
Maybe buy a nice rug
And breathe.

my one among the millions

I will take a million steps forward
Despite the pull of you urging me back

I will take a million breaths
Even if the air feels stale without you in it

I will love a million new people
Despite my heart aching for you with every beat

I will cross a million mountaintops and through a million rivers
Even if I can feel every atom that separates us

I will think a million thoughts that aren't about you
Despite every other one being about you

I will wake to see a million new sunrises
Even if my first thought is you and not the sun

I will make a million wishes upon the stars
Despite my impulse to always wish for you

I will live a million lives without you
Even if I loved the one with you the most.

strength

I find so much strength in pain
When the weight of the world
Crashes down upon me
And drags me low to the ground
My soul comes alive
And bounces back with a force
That would level that world to dust.
But that would never happen.
Because in that calm before my perfect storm
I find the mercy that the world did not give me.
I find a deep love for myself
That far surpasses the love that I have been shown
Because in that moment when I lay face full of ground
It was my own hand that lifted me from the shadows of my
pain.

our quantum entanglement

The one who could read my heart
From light years away
The Big Bang of my existence
A collected source of entropy

A glorious nebula
That collects worthless dust
And turns them into life
Into stars

Like the cosmos, you are always there
Full of secrets
Bound by wisdom
And radiating unconditional love

We are the same particle
Entangled
Only to assume our places upon perception
Eternally bonded

Part Three: The Ending that Came

A STORY OF ACCEPTANCE

gold

You were gold.
You were sunlit beaches and golden eyes
Early mornings in the bright sun
Hands moving slow on olive skin
And candlelit nights in a new country.

You were so gold
That I actually mistook you for the sun
And thought that I may die without you
And never see another day
If you weren't there to illuminate my path.

But then I got used to the night
And the dark became beautiful
And the moon shone a light onto my path
And I always found my way back home.

But every now and then
I see the golden glow of a street light intruding on my way
And for a fleeting moment
I think of you, my golden one.

forever young

Forever young with you
In the corners of my mind
Forever confused and hazy
Drunk on wine and passion
Secretly intertwined
The taste of sin on your lips
Before you found your shame

Forever young and free
Endless nights on dark highways
Moonlight in my hair
And your hands upon my thighs
No lessons were learned that night
Our souls too busy yearning

Forever young and in love
Your eyes burn into mine
Enthralled and exhilarated
Just at the sight of you
You held me so tightly
As if you could melt yourself into me
And become one
And never to be parted

Forever young and frozen
Never to see me age
Never to finish the story
And never to return again
Forever wondering
What we could have been
Forever stuck upon
The memory of what we were.

too much

Was my love too sweet for you to handle?
Was that taste too addictive for you?
Like a dark wine at midnight
Or ripened strawberries
In the sunshine

Did I love you too strongly?
Did I grip your soul too tightly?
A bond fortified by flames
Melted soul into soul
And hardened by time

Was my touch too soft for you?
Was the bliss too all-consuming?
My kiss too gentle and warm
And the way I held your heart
Was too safe

Did I understand you too completely?
Did I know your mind too well?
I drew too many maps
To the corners of your mind
A well traversed path

Were we too perfect together?
Did our souls meld too well?
Two kindred spirits
In beautiful harmony
Both perfected and flawed

the keeper

I am the keeper
Keeper of the keys
To everyone's hearts
The protector, the guardian
The bodyguard without a choice

I am the guide
Guide through everyone's own journey
Including mine
Crafting maps of emotional intelligence
Showing everyone the way back home

I am the mother
Mother of lost souls
A mother bird
And beneath my wings, it is overcrowded
A nest with no room to breathe
Or spread my own wings

I am the fountain
Fountain where all come to drink
It will never run empty
A cycle in the sky replenishes
And though it may feel used
It knows that it is needed.

holier than thou

What a perfect angel you are.
How perfectly holy and perfectly moral
A man who does not know sin
Because he simply closes his eyes while he commits it.

What a man you are.
So true to your word and honest
A man whose tongue has never formed lies or spewed hatred
Because it's apparently God's tongue, not his.

I clap my hands for you.
Congratulations on earning the sole seat in Heaven
Only because you cut in line
And then burned all the other chairs.

I am so proud of you.
You figured it out
You solved all the secrets of the universe
Because the truth was always whatever fit your narrative.

When you make it to heaven without me
And I'm burning in hell with everyone else
Let God know that I'm sorry
But paradise with you was too lonely.

thank you (pt 1)

To the one who gives me purpose
By appreciating the beauty and meaning of each day
A childlike curiosity from the wisest soul I know

To the one who protects me from the shadows
Because you exist as the most brilliant beam of sun
A sunset and sunrise in one person

To the one who soothes my sorrows
By cradling my heart like a rib cage
Rocking me from dusk to dawn to dusk

To the one who taught me joy in its purest form
By recognizing the delicate perfection of our world
Starting each day in a state of euphoric awe

To the one who gave me freedom
Carrying me for miles to my new home
Breaking my chains by disproving their existence

To the one who understands me best
The boundlessness of my heart and fire in my soul
Loving every part and mending every need

To the one who hears the music in my laugh
And could write a symphony on its tone
Delicate notes on gentle days

To the one who pushes me further
Through mountaintops and valleys that I could have never crossed
Exploring peaks and caverns of my potential

Thank you to me.
I was my savior all along.

I thought it was you

I thought it was you
The one who lights my soul on fire
Who sings in tune with my heart
And takes me back to a home beyond this world
The one whose tongue speaks poetry
Poetry inspired by my eyes
But spoken with actions just the same
Whose gaze holds mine when hands cannot
With a spirit in black and white like my own

I thought it was you
Who could read my story
And feel moved by the words
Not just a memorization of me
But an understanding
A firm grasp of what it means to be divine

I thought it was you
Who would be the sweetest song I'd hear
A cacophony of notes
That could never be organized
In a symphony that I would understand
Your song would fall upon deaf ears
Because your lyrics were never true

I thought it was you.
I wanted it to be you.
It couldn't be you.
But if not you, then who?

crossroad

Though we weathered together
Through perilous lands and endless trials
Through sunset islands and flowery meadows
But here we stand at last
our path diverges into two
and you do not hesitate to head left
and I do not hesitate to head right
I look back and hope you're waiting there
I look left and hope we're parallel here
I look ahead and know you've moved too quick for me
Fading away into the obscurity of the future
Not waiting, not parallel, and nowhere for me to see.

thank you (pt 2)

Thank you to the universe
For overruling my manifestations.

Hopelessly romantic pleas
Begging for chains
Stockholm syndrome of the heart
A sentencing of my own designs
I asked you to behead me in the courtyard
And instead you gave me a throne.

Thank you to the universe
For rejecting my prayers.

My palace built on dust
An illusion of wishful thinking
All came crashing down
A hazy cloud of smoke and truths revealed
Leaving me with nothing
And the irony that this is what I always had.

Thank you to the universe
For taking away what did not serve me.

I wanted to love you.
wanted to rest
your tired head
to mend the scratches
on your soul
so restless and afraid
and so hopelessly ashamed
I wanted to fan the flames
of the fire
that is your soul
I wanted to also soothe
that fire
to extinguish
and to sleep
to rest those weary eyes
and know that you are okay
I wanted to love you
and I almost did.
I wanted you to let me
and you almost did.

dreams

If all that we see
Is just a dream in a dream
Then where is that lucidity that I crave?

For when I sleep, my soul grabs the reigns
Finding footing on an astral plane
And guiding my dreams to a paradise

But in this waking dream
Though I feel dreamy and dazed all the same
The manifestation is always delayed

How can I dream better
In this dream within a dream?
Where do I find the control?

In endless days and nights
I lay dreaming but awake
Watching the scenes slip by

But in the those nights on an astral plane
My higher self takes hold
And here, I can only observe.

the last time

No more nights where we're together
No slow mornings by your side
It was our last day for forever
And we didn't even know this time

We didn't know that was our last kiss
The last time I felt you close
The last dance under the covers
The last taste of wine from my lips

We'll never again have those moments
Of guilty worship of one another
Laying down our defenses
And falling deep into your eyes

No more whispered nothings
No sweet promises of tomorrow
The foundation came crumbling down
And I was too distracted by you

I lost my last piece of you.
I can't build a life out of dust.
This is the last life with you.
So I let you go, my love.

the performer

If home is where the heart is,
For now, it's in my pocket
Safely tucked away
And shielded from the world

I used to store her on a podium
Open for business
Come one, come all
And they traveled for miles to marvel at her

But the heavy traffic wore her down
Leaving cracks and deep imprints
Eroded with time and from action
And she was retired from the show

It took so long to mend her scars
To show her that she was worth that care
But she was healed
But also completely transformed

And so my heart is kept close to me
And I show her the love that she deserves
I wait for the one who deserves her
The only one to break my fear and expose her to the world again

I don't owe you anything

I don't owe you anything.

I don't owe you my sweet energy.
That you so greedily desire
Just to drain the well dry
And then complain that you are thirsty.

I don't owe you my patience.
My unconditional understanding
Is only for the lucky ones
Who I have deemed worthy of my grace.

I don't owe you my sympathy.
It is not efficient nor fair
That I am expected to bear my own cross entirely
And then pick up the deadweight of yours.

I don't owe you my spark.
I vow that I will never again
Dim the light that burns throughout me
To make you feel more comfortable.

I don't owe you my spirit.
That carefree enjoyment and childlike wonder
That you need to get through your boring days everyday
Because you bring down my vibration to compensate for yours.

I hope that in my absence
You will notice that all the things you sought from me
Were just aspects that you were lacking in yourself
And I never owed you anything.

rest

Weary girl,
rest your eyes.
Find comfort in the darkness.
that you no longer fear
for you have known it
far too long.
Relax your shoulders
and let those tears escape you,
hot and heavy down your cheek
they burn with relief.
All that you have held so tight
choking and suffocating you.
Breathe, dear one.
exhale all those memories
that nip at you in the night.
There is no night.
Just the velvet darkness
of rest and of sleep.
Welcome it, loved one.

Part Four: The Beginning to Come

A STORY OF REBIRTH

let me love you

Lie awake with me
In a kingdom by the sea
Or a studio apartment in a noisy city
Lay with me and let the moonlight bathe us
Silver glow upon golden feelings
Warm and burning in the cold morning hours
Drunk and high off one another
Unsure if waking or dreaming
Your personal Aphrodite lay beside you
Steady hands tracing tickled skin
Soft kisses pacing a map across your body
Feel your heartbeat outrace your shaky breaths, my dear
And fall in sync with mine
Let me love you so tenderly here
I wait for you in this hypothetical state of bliss, my dear
A separate dimension and ahead of you in time.

burn

I want to be engulfed in the fire that is you
Burning through my core until I feel alive again
Lost in a smoky haze
And unable to escape
The air so thick with my being
Matter spread through the atmosphere
Hoping desperately to mingle with the matter that is you
Fall upon me hot and heavy
Flames flicking like a tongue
And singeing the skin where you've been
Tastes of spice fill the air between us
Burning and aching in my lungs
Let the flames engulf our worlds
Burning down all that we've built
I would submit it all to you
To burn beneath your passion
And let the smoke carry me on to the heavens.

incarnation

I touch down upon the Earth
Fallen angel without a sound
Only a melodic cry as I step into this carbon life

Over and over again
I swallow my pride
And I allow ignorance to overtake me
I accept ego's grasp
And I breathe oxygen in this garden of the stars
So vulnerable and afraid
But curious and pure

We do this every time
Willfully lost in a sea of emotions
And war, and chaos, and greed
But reaching equal heights of pure beauty
Because that's what we embody
And that's our gift to the earth

Here I am again.
Lost but finding my way to you
A map guided only by my heart
I wait for you, my dear
For our rendezvous on this earthly plane.

Honey, I'm home.

moonlight

Lover with the touch as light as a feather
Shining as a delicate moon beam
With a stillness as fragile as hummingbird bones
Let a gentle breeze carry you home to me

Touch my heart so sweetly
Cast your shadow upon me in silver moon light
Soften your gaze in crystal blue eyes
And find your heartbeat softening with mine

My heart needs a tender lover
And my soul needs gentle hands
Callused from your own devotions
In need of a soft and kindred spirit
Love me lightly and love me truly
Whisper of inspirations of me
And let me feel your breath upon me
Gentle winds of sweet promises

my midas touch

My Midas touch
A touch of gold to your heart
Sunshine deep into your bones
And bringing value to your life

Divinity beyond cognition
A frequency incomprehensible
But felt deeply in the soul
Bringing you closer to the sun
But never burning
Only warming

My Midas touch
Turning you to gold
A glimmer of glory
A promise of security
Woven in golden strands

bloom

This bud of love
That I grew into a beauteous flower
Watered by tears
And dried in the sunshine
Waiting for you in the springtime.

But for now, I sow the seeds
Breathing life and beauty into the bloom
A hearty stock that will soon grow fruitful
But for now, decorates the earth in bloom
Never harvested, only admired.

Wind may come and disrupt the stillness
Sending the bloom astray
But the generosity of the bloom is never ending
And the earth is bathed in color.

gentle souls

Oh, gentle soul
Moonlight on your hair
And pomegranate on your lips
Stay here with me
At home in the hypothetical
Lost with you in a realm before our time

Each night as we lay sleeping
And our higher selves move beyond this plane
When the pieces of us form back together
Reunited in our astral home
Where we dance in the stars
Until the sun shines on our earthly bodies

You won't remember me in the morning
Not the shine of my hair
Or the sweetness of my touch
But you will wake with the feeling of me
The knowing that there is a love out there for you
Waiting, and unconditional
And soon you will know me.

And I, you.

full moon

My earth has been cast into darkness
A hallowing sense of dread fills the air
And I am scared,

I am scared that I will not find my way home in this darkness
That the darkness has become my home
That even the stars cannot guide me,

It is so dark that I cannot see my hands before my eyes
Making me forget who I was
If I was even a person in the first place,

I fall to my knees upon the cold ground
And I close my eyes even though it is dark
My mind suddenly becomes calm and my heart begins to slow,

A light forms within me
Showing me who I was, who I am, and who I will be
Illuminated there in my mind's eye,

I open my eyes in this physical realm
And there, so glorious upon the horizon
Was a full moon that illuminated the entire earth with a silver
glow,

My pain, my fear, my animosity
Turned into a brilliance of my own creation
Abundantly full and eager to guide my way home.

winds of change

The winds of change are howling
Tossing me in directions
To worlds that I would have never ventured.

I feel weightless
Lost and stuck in time
Unsure of where I will land.

At first I was terrified
As if my fear and assumptions
Could direct me to a safer landing.

But I just kept flying
Not falling or crashing
Cradled by an unseen force.

And then I let go
I let the winds take me farther
Indifferent to where I would land.

In my utter lack of control
A calming hush befell me
And I started to trust the wind.

I'm still there flying
Watching potential lands come and go
Realizing those lands were never for me.

The wind still takes me further
And when I land, I will build a home
But for now, I enjoy the view.

energy

My energy is so addictive
A cosmic cocktail of stardust and seduction
Lips like rose filled valleys
Eyes like a mirage of endless oceans
And hands that hold an unknown soft power
Reminding you of a home that you can't remember

I am an ethereal goddess
Hell bent on this earthly experience
Divine connection in my aura
I hold your gentle souls
And I guide your paths lovingly
To become your highest selves
I know you better than you know me

I shine with the power of infinite suns
And I soothe with the energy of the mother moon
I amplify the beauty of every earthly sunset
And I unleash the wisdom of higher realms

My energy is pure enlightenment
Manifestation is for the birds
I lay on the crossroad of the past and future
Relishing in the collective shift to come

man on the moon

I wait for the man on the moon
Someone who would travel through space to find me
Who spotted me from a planet far away
And thought that I was perfect
Who saw my beauty from a distant land
And chose me over all the stars
The one who would never change me
Who could never even imagine a better design

I want for the man on the moon
A solitary figure in the cosmos
Someone so unique
That they stand above the heavens
With a soul that shapes the tides
And inspires centuries of tales

I love for the man on the moon
The one who would understand
The isolation despite constant adoration
Who comes to me despite great distances
Confident in our gravitational pull

red string

I know that this romantic soul of mine
Would never have stepped an angelic toe upon this earth
Without the knowledge of the greatest romance story to come
Without an assurance that a great love awaited
Without the presence of a promising red string

I tried to trace the origin of the red string upon me
Knowing from the pull that there must be an end
And though the string became tangled
In knots that shouldn't have been
I released myself and found footing
To begin tracing that string again

So though I may be romantic
I will never be hopeless

high priestess

Though I have walked through the valley
Of the shadow of death
I have greeted evil as an old friend
As someone who does not scare me
Someone childish who I have moved beyond

I hear the call of the void
And my soul does not stir
Because I know that the void only exists
In reflection of all the abundance that is
That the power of loss lies in love

The dark night of my soul
Turned into the dark era
And in that shadow, I learned how to create light
I realized that the sun will not rise
If I stopped trusting that it would

I am powerful because I have known fear
I am beautiful because I have explored my ugly
I am wise because I have done wrong
I am glorious because I know my shadow

out of body

Who am I in this world
If not a figment of a divine imagination
An impulsive wish of the universe
To exist in this simple carbon form
A glorious day dream of hypothetical being
A guilty pleasure of the cosmos

This ego of mine is my own creation
Crafted lovingly by a higher power
Molded from stardust into perfection
I am my soul's romanticization of humanity
Its favorite combination of genes
The main character of my cosmic saga

My existence on this plane
Is validated
By my existence on this plane
I am the the greatest love story of the universe
The "what if" of consciousness
And all the incredible perfection that followed

the garden

What a paradise this is
This garden in the stars
Where we grow and play
Making mistakes to become better
Cosmic children learning how to love

What an oasis this is
Our earth that the universe chose as our home
This incubator of life
Our own personal nebula
Raising us into stars

What a heaven we have on earth
Its beauty is what we have made of it
Natural wonders and man made communities
Nothing more than a colony of ants
Living lives on our grassy rock

Epilogue

letter to God

Hey God, it's me again.
I'm glad we've been keeping in touch lately.

I just wanted to say thanks. For not giving up on me. Not that you would. But I almost did. I almost gave up on me and you. But I didn't. Was that you?

I just don't understand it. What is this? What am I? What are you? I'm looking at this tree and I don't know what it could be. If it could be your hands reaching out to us. Or sensors of the earth. Or an ancient being here to gather our sorrow and guide our hearts. Or maybe it's just a tree. Or even an illusion. I feel like those who just see a tree have their eyes closed and are blind. Maybe mine are open. I see an endless stream of possibilities when I see that tree.

And what is next? I'm so transfixed on a tree that the thought of my death is far from the reach of my consciousness. I can't imagine there being a concrete and distinguished answer on the other side. As if one group is right, and the other is wrong. It must be more abstract than that. And something that I will never understand.

But if nothing else, it's beautiful. This world. I'm watching leaves dance through the sky and a dragonfly float around them. Maybe that's the comfort. That's the solace of living a life of ignorance and confusion and the sin of being awake to recognize it. It doesn't matter. Because it's still beautiful.

I dream of my existence as an epic tale as the savior of the earth. Something reminiscent of an action story with a fantasy twist that I would have read cover to cover in my adolescence. It's odd that I crave such a story of greatness while at the same time begging the universe for peace and serenity. No novel or hero's journey creates growth from peace. It comes from conflict. Maybe I'm not great. But I'm surely not mundane. My life has never been an epic, but a poem.

A poem of death, cold, and heartbreak.
Of beauty, of rebirth.
Of intimacy and of war.
Loving, leaving, trusting, believing.
Tears of joy and frustration and love and pain.
Of the absolute deepest depths of humanity, the raw power of emotions.
And chaos, chaos, chaos, chaos, chaos.

Maybe that's the answer.

Thanks for listening, God. Until the next time.